LOGOS CURSIVE
Book 2: Proverbs and Sayings

Published by Logos Press
an imprint of Canon Press
P.O. Box 8729, Moscow, Idaho 83843
800.488.2034 | logospressonline.com

B.J. Loyd, *Logos Cursive, Book 2: Proverbs and Sayings*
Copyright © 2020 by B.J. Loyd. Assembly sayings used by permission of Matt Whitling

Cover design by James Engerbretson.
Interior design by Valerie Anne Bost.

Printed in the United States of America.

All rights reserved. No part of this publication may be reproduced, stored in a retrieval system, or transmitted in any form by any means, electronic, mechanical, photocopy, recording, or otherwise, without prior permission of the author, except as provided by USA copyright law.

Unless otherwise noted, Bible quotations are from The ESV® Bible (The Holy Bible, English Standard Version®), copyright © 2001 by Crossway, a publishing ministry of Good News Publishers. Used by permission. All rights reserved. / Bible quotations noted as BSB are from The Holy Bible, Berean Study Bible, BSB, copyright ©2016, 2018 by Bible Hub, Used by Permission. All Rights Reserved Worldwide. / Bible quotations noted as NKJV are from the New King James Version®, copyright ©1982 by Thomas Nelson, Inc. Used by permission. All rights reserved. / Bible quotations noted as KJV are from the King James Version®, public domain.

Library of Congress Cataloging-in-Publication Data forthcoming.

20 21 22 23 24 25 26 27 28 29   10 9 8 7 6 5 4 3 2 1

Logos Cursive
Book 2: Proverbs and Sayings

B.J. LOYD

with Assembly Sayings by MATT WHITLING

AN IMPRINT OF CANON PRESS | MOSCOW, IDAHO

Schedule

Dear Teacher,

Welcome to *Logos Cursive, Book 2: Proverbs and Sayings.* This schedule will help your second graders continue their cursive learning over the course of a semester doing one lesson per weekday (or over the course of a year, if you practice two to three times per week).

   This book provides a fun twist to copy work from longtime Logos School principal Matt Whitling. At the school's weekly assemblies, Mr. Whitling will call out the first part of a saying, and the students will enthusiastically shout back the response. Many of the assembly sayings are taken from the book of Proverbs, but Mr. Whitling has thrown in a few other memorable quotes for good measure. If you want to try shouting them, say the part before the ellipsis (…) and have your student(s) shout back the rest.

   Some of the sayings are very short, so students are to copy them multiple times. Help them be aware of that instruction.

WEEK	ASSIGNMENT
1	Exercises 1–4
2	Exercises 5–9
3	Exercises 10–13
4	Exercises 14–18
5	Exercises 19–22
6	Exercises 23–27
7	Exercises 28–31
8	Exercises 32–36
9	Exercises 37–40
10	Exercises 41–44
11	Exercises 45–49
12	Exercises 50–53
13	Exercises 54–58
14	Exercises 59–62
15	Exercises 63–67
16	Exercises 68–71

Name: _____

Trace and then neatly copy.

The fear of the Lord

is the beginning

of knowledge; fools

despise wisdom and

instruction. Proverbs 1:7

Name: _____

Trace and then neatly copy.

Don't... whine.

Don't... complain.

Don't... make

excuses, sir!

John Wooden's father

Name: _____

Trace and then neatly copy.

Finish . . .

strong — as to the Lord

and not to men.

from Colossians 3:23

Book 2: Proverbs and Sayings   Exercise 3

Name: _____

Trace and then neatly copy.

A soft answer turns

away wrath...

but a harsh word stirs

up anger. Proverbs 15:1

Name: _____

Trace and then **neatly copy four times**.

Never . . . panic.

Book 2: Proverbs and Sayings

Exercise 5

Trace and then neatly copy.

Like vinegar to the teeth... and smoke to the eyes, so is the sluggard to those who send him. Proverbs 10:26

Name: _____

Trace and then neatly copy.

After class...

thank your teacher,

thank your teacher,

thank your teacher.

Book 2: Proverbs and Sayings

Exercise 7

Name: _____

Trace and then neatly copy.

Train up a child in

the way he should

go . . . even when he is

old he will not depart

from it. Proverbs 22:6

Name: _____

Trace and then neatly copy.

Hand . . . shake —

firm and cheerful,

eyes on eyes!

Book 2: Proverbs and Sayings   Exercise 9

Name: _____

Trace and then neatly copy.

A friend loves at all

times... and a brother

is born for adversity.

Proverbs 17:17

Name: _____

Trace and then **neatly copy two times**.

Leave it . . . better than

you found it.

Name: _____

Trace and then **neatly copy four times.**

Hustle . . . to help out.

Name: _____

Trace and then neatly copy.

Students . . .

gratitude, sacrifice,

excellence; thankfully

giving my best.

(From the Logos School motto.)

Name: _____

Trace and then neatly copy.

Obey . . .

right away, all the

way, and with a good

attitude every day.

Name: _____

Trace and then neatly copy.

If you fall down…

smile and keep on

playing.

Book 2: Proverbs and Sayings

Name: _____

Trace and then neatly copy.

Whoever is slow to

anger . . .

is better than the

mighty,

and he who rules his

Exercise 16   Logos Cursive

spirit...

than he who takes a

city. Proverbs 16:32

Trace and then neatly copy.

Those who are faithful

with little . . .

will be faithful with

much.

from Luke 16:10

Name: _____

Trace and then neatly copy.

Remember...

I am a great sinner.

Remember...

Christ is a great Savior.

Name: _____

Trace and then neatly copy.

God opposes the

proud...

but gives grace to the

humble.

from James 4:6

Name: _____

Trace and then neatly copy.

Not unto us, O Lord,

Not unto us . . .

But unto thy name

give glory. Psalm 115:1

(KJV. From the Logos School song.)

Name: _____

Trace and then neatly copy.

He who hates

correction . . .

is stupid. Proverbs 12:1

(NKJV)

Exercise 21 — Logos Cursive

Name: _____

Trace and then neatly copy.

Every word of God

proves true; he is a

shield to those who

take refuge in him.

Proverbs 30:5

Name: _____

Trace and then neatly copy.

How do . . .

I win that race?

from I Corinthians 9:24

Name: _____

Trace and then neatly copy.

I will stay in prison…

till the moss grows

on my eye lids rather

than disobey God.

John Bunyan

Book 2: Proverbs and Sayings

Name: _____

Trace and then **neatly copy two times**.

Be a truth teller . . .

even when it hurts.

Exercise 25

Logos Cursive

Name: _____

Trace and then neatly copy.

Charm is deceitful, and

beauty is vain, but a

woman who fears the

Lord is to be praised.

Proverbs 31.30

Name: _____

Trace and then neatly copy.

I knew that you are

a gracious God and

merciful . . .

slow to anger and

abounding in steadfast

love, and relenting

from disaster. Jonah 4:2

Name: _____

Trace and then neatly copy.

He who exalts

himself...

will be humbled,

and he who humbles

himself...

will be exalted.

Luke 14:11

Name: _____

Trace and then neatly copy.

Have I not

commanded you? Be

strong and be

courageous. Do not be

frightened, and do not

be dismayed . . . for the

Lord your God is with

you, wherever you go.

Joshua 1:9

Name: _____

Trace and then neatly copy.

Courage is . . .

strength in the face of

danger or difficulty.

Name: _____

Trace and then neatly copy.

A joyful heart is good

medicine... but a

crushed spirit dries up

the bones.

Proverbs 17:22

Name: _____

Trace and then **neatly copy two times**.

The bigger they are . . .

the harder they fall.

Exercise 32   Logos Cursive

Name: _____

Trace and then neatly copy.

If one gives an

answer before he

hears . . . it is his folly

and shame.

Proverbs 18:13

Book 2: Proverbs and Sayings

Name: _____

Trace and then neatly copy.

What God loves . . .

I love.

What God hates . . .

I hate.

Exercise 34 — Logos Cursive

Name: _____

Trace and then neatly copy.

A wise son makes his

father glad…

but a foolish man

despises his mother.

Proverbs 15:20

Trace and then neatly copy.

Answer not a fool according to his folly . . . lest you be like him yourself.

Answer a fool according

Exercise 36

Logos Cursive

to his folly...

lest he be wise in his

own eyes.

Proverbs 26:4-5

Name: _____

Trace and then neatly copy.

Rebuke a wise man

and . . .

he will love you.

Proverbs 9:8

(NKJV)

Name: _____

Trace and then neatly copy.

What do you have…

that you did not

receive?

1 Corinthians 4:7

Name: _____

Trace and then neatly copy.

Do . . .

as you would be done

by. As you would be

done by, do.

Exercise 39   Logos Cursive

Name: _____

Trace and then **neatly copy three times.**

Work hard...

work smart.

Name: _____

Trace and then neatly copy.

Iron sharpens

iron ... and one man

sharpens another.

Proverbs 27:17

Name: _____

Trace and then **neatly copy two times.**

Manners are . . .

love in trifles.

Name: _____

Trace and then neatly copy.

The sluggard buries his

hand in the dish...

and will not even

bring it back to his

mouth. Proverbs 19:24

Trace and then neatly copy.

Mistakes? . . .

Laugh at your own,

not your neighbor's.

Book 2: Proverbs and Sayings

Name: _____

Trace and then neatly copy.

The rich rules over

the poor . . . and the

borrower is the slave of

the lender.

Proverbs 22:7

Name: _____

Trace and then neatly copy.

Are you ready to strike

your colors? I have

not yet begun to fight!

John Paul Jones

Name: _____

Trace and then **neatly copy two times**.

Esther said . . .

"If I perish, I perish."

Esther 4:16

Trace and then neatly copy.

Gratitude? . . .

Thankful for what

Jesus has done for us.

Book 2: Proverbs and Sayings

Exercise 48

Name: _____

Trace and then neatly copy.

Sacrifice? . . .

Take up your cross

and follow Him.

from Luke 9:23

Name: _____

Trace and then neatly copy.

Excellence? . . .

Do it heartily, as to

the Lord and not to

men.

from Colossians 3:23

Name: _____

Trace and then neatly copy.

My talents are . . .

not my own.

Take your talents and

. . . double them.

from Matthew 25

Name: _____

Trace and then neatly copy.

Wisdom . . .

is more precious than

rubies.

from Proverbs 3:15

Name: _____

Trace and then neatly copy.

Bright stars . . .

don't grumble or

complain.

from Philippians 2:14-15

Name: _____

Trace and then neatly copy.

Better is a dry morsel

with quiet . . .

than a house full of

feasting with strife.

Proverbs 17:1

Name: _____

Trace and then neatly copy.

Let a man meet a she-

bear robbed of her cubs

rather than a fool in

his folly. Proverbs 17:12

Name: _____

Trace and then neatly copy.

The ant works hard . . .

without a coach.

from Proverbs 6:6

(NKJV)

Book 2: Proverbs and Sayings

Name: _____

Trace and then neatly copy.

Jesus said, "As you did

it to one of the least of

these my brothers . . .

you did it to me."

from Matthew 25:40

Name: _____

Trace and then neatly copy.

Like a gold ring in a

pig's snout . . .

is a beautiful woman

without discretion.

Proverbs 11:22

Name: _____

Trace and then neatly copy.

The generous soul . . .

will be made rich.

Proverbs 11:25

(NKJV)

Name: _____

Trace and then neatly copy.

Greater love has no one than this... that he lay down his life for his friends.

John 15:13

(BSB)

Book 2: Proverbs and Sayings

Exercise 60

Name: _____

Trace and then neatly copy.

Go to the ant, you

sluggard . . .

consider its ways and

be wise. Proverbs 6:6

Name: _____

Trace and then **neatly copy two times**.

The bigger they are . . .

the harder they fall.

Name: _____

Trace and then neatly copy.

Whoever conceals his

transgressions . . .

will not prosper,

but he who confesses

and forsakes them . . .

will obtain mercy.

Proverbs 28:13

Trace and then neatly copy.

Out of the abundance

of the heart...

the mouth speaks.

Matthew 12:34

Name: _____

Trace and then neatly copy.

I am . . . better than I

deserve to be,

but not . . . as well as

I hope to be.

Richard Baxter

Name: _____

Trace and then neatly copy.

Trust in the Lord with

all your heart... and

do not lean on your

own understanding.

Proverbs 3:5

Name: _____

Trace and then neatly copy.

There are six things

that the Lord hates,

seven that are an

abomination to him:

Proverbs 6:16

Book 2: Proverbs and Sayings

Exercise 68

Name: _____

Trace and then neatly copy.

haughty eyes, a lying

tongue, and hands that

shed innocent blood,

Proverbs 6:17

Name: _____

Trace and then neatly copy.

a heart that devises

wicked plans, feet that

make haste to run to

evil,

Proverbs 6:18

Name: _____

Trace and then neatly copy.

a false witness who

breathes out lies, and

one who sows discord

among brothers.

Proverbs 6:19

www.ingramcontent.com/pod-product-compliance
Lightning Source LLC
Chambersburg PA
CBHW050456110426
42743CB00017B/3381